SALES WATER'S

20 POINT SYSTEM ✔

20pointsystem.com

Introduction

This small book was written to share the most requested secret of my career. When other sales professionals, new hires, managers, and even people in other industries hear about it, they are always intrigued and usually request more information. "Can you send me that 20-Point System you use?"

I did not invent the system. The 20-Point System was shared from a platform in a hotel meeting room. I was young and eager to figure out what I needed to learn so I could pay my bills and survive my first few years in a commission-based business.

In 2003, I had less than a year in the financial services industry. I went to an association meeting in Milwaukee, Wisconsin, and I was desperately hoping to get some ideas—or even one idea—on how to improve my business. An older gentleman, who was one of the speakers, had qualified for one of the industry's top production standards: Million Dollar Round Table® (MDRT®). I had been to many meetings and listened to many people, some of whom I knew were not making much money. Qualifying for MDRT® meant this guy was making six figures. I was not, so I listened. He said that if you use the 20-Point System that there would be no question, "you will be tripping over MDRT before the end of the year." I believed him.

More importantly, I wrote it down. He described the 20-Points System briefly. It really was not that complicated. He did not describe the system very extensively. It was not the point of his talk, just a small side note, but I caught it. He said that if you used it, it worked, and then he moved on.

I went to work to define the system more thoroughly. I wrote down some different definitions and reasons for awarding myself points, and I started using it.

CHAPTER 1

The 20-Point System & How To Use It

20-POINT SYSTEM

Here are the key result activities to track:

» Making a call and getting told no: **1 point**

» Making a call and getting told yes: **2 points**

» Getting stood up for an appointment: **3 points**

» Having an appointment: **4 points**

» Making a sale: **5 points**

DEFINITIONS

1. **Getting told no:** You have to be calling a client or potential customer and asking for a pre-sale interview: delivery attempts, answering machines, and wrong numbers don't count. You have to be speaking to a live person you want to sit down with and get them to either say, "Call me back," "I'll call you back," or saying flat-out "No." That and only that is one point. If you make 50 phone calls and no one is home, you get zero points.

2. **Getting told yes:** You need to be calling for an appointment to make a sale in the future. The same criteria for getting told no applies. You need to be calling to meet with a client for a review, an initial appointment, or a closing interview. Those pre-sale appointment calls are worth two points, if the person agrees to a meeting. This can also be done face to face.

3. **Getting stood up:** This is not a reschedule or a cancel. This is an appointment you are stood up for. You have to drive to the location or be in your office when the appointment is to begin and actually get stiffed by the client. This seems unproductive, but the system works.

4. **Having an appointment:** This is, again, not paperwork delivery, follow up, service call, or an appointment to "drop in" and sign a form. This is you asking questions and performing the process to move towards a sale.

5. **Making a sale:** This should be self-explanatory. You must collect a check or sign paperwork for a purchase. You should be able to say, "Thank you for your business."

HOW TO TRACK

Write this on your daily schedule and fill in as needed:

» NO – 1, 1, 1   » APPT – 4, 4

» YES – 2, 2   » SALE – 5

» STOOD – 3

23 points – GREAT DAY! You had four potential appointments and one sale, and a few calls. This process daily is very productive.

The 20-Point System is simple. Anyone can understand it, and properly motivated, anyone can get 20 points in a day. The 20-Point System is a daily accountability system of tracking your customer calls and meetings. It is a simple program of consistency. The objective is to use it every day, in good times and bad.

If I offered you $1,000, to get your 20 points by 5 pm, you would probably be done by noon and looking for your money. Most people need a manager to tell them to get back to work. This clearly is not for you. If you are willing to work hard, without oversight, the 20-Point System will allow you to measure the things that assure your monthly income. This program takes the anxiety out of commission-based income. If consistently used, the 20-Point System will drive you to the top of your company, and industry, faster than you can imagine. Before we define more thoroughly, what the 20-Point System is, let us discuss why and how it works.

STARTING OUT AND THE SOPHOMORE SLUMP

I credit the 20-Point System for sustaining my career. This system was crucial back in the beginning: in the first few years and through my sophomore slump. The *sophomore slump* is when you have called everyone that you know in your natural market (friends and family mostly). At that point, you need to figure out how to generate new business and referrals from the general public. You need to call on people that you have no relationship with. You have to go out and talk to strangers and try to convince them that you are someone worth doing business with.

As you probably know, this is a difficult endeavor for a new, inexperienced, unconfident sales person. The 20-Point System does not work right away. The day you start using the 20-Point System, the momentum is not there. It's like shoveling coal into the boiler of a locomotive.

THE LOCOMOTIVE EFFECT

First, you start shoveling coal for the boiler to heat up. You work, but nothing happens. Eventually, the fire gets hot and the steam pressure builds. Then the locomotive starts moving. It doesn't speed up quickly. There is a train to pull, which is moving people through your prospect funnel. There is an enormous amount of lag time. There is so much lag time that most people decide it is not working and quit.

The more you consistently shovel the coal into the boiler of the locomotive, the faster it goes. Eventually, usually in a month or two (yes, two months), you have developed serious momentum. If you have been shoveling coal for 30 to 60 days, using the 20-Point System, your locomotive is flying down the tracks. You stand up from shoveling coal, stretch your back, count some of the money rolling in, and pay some bills. Then it happens: the delusion.

MISTAKEN CONFIDENCE

All of that activity keeps that locomotive going and doesn't allow you to run out of steam right away or lose too much speed. You have been working hard and deserve a break, so you stop shoveling coal into the locomotive. You have the sales activity, prospects, and opportunities in your sales funnel. Just like a schizophrenic who thinks he is cured, you stop taking your medicine. You feel ok for some time while your previous activity pays deferred dividends, but just like that mentally-ill patient, trouble is brewing for you.

BUILDING OR ERODING DISCIPLINE

When you fall out of the habit of shoveling coal or you take a little break, your locomotive doesn't stop immediately, but you have lost personal momentum. Every discipline supports every other discipline. But every lack of discipline fuels more of the same. This is similar to breaking your diet. You agree to that one piece of cake. Now, eating a couple more cookies is that much easier. You already broke your discipline. Or, when a man becomes desperate and robs a store, robbing the second store on his crime spree is not nearly as difficult. He has already defied his conscience.

> ## Every discipline supports every other discipline.

In the same way, once you decide to go to the gym to lift some weights, getting on the treadmill and doing your cardio is that much easier. Most people don't go to the gym once every two weeks. They either go consistently or not at all. People usually do not have disciplines that are widely segmented by time yet still consistent. Your sales activity is the same. Once you fall out of the habit, it is progressively more difficult to find new motivation to persist as time passes.

If you, for an extended period of time, do not shovel coal into the locomotive, that train will slow down. Your sales funnel and your activity funnel will continue to diminish. It's an easy trap to get sucked into in a sales career. Another problem with diminished activity and diminished sales is that, many times, your income, which also has a lag time, has a delayed reaction, fooling you into a comfortable place and into the career danger zone.

THE CAREER DANGER ZONE

Figure 1.1 shows that when you are doing high levels of activity, it is usually because you do not have much money. That is real motivation. Once you start receiving income, your natural tendency is to ease back on the activity. When the money drops off, you realize you have to increase your activity. This is where sales people get to the point where they must ask themselves, "Can I dig deep within myself for new enthusiasm?" You know you need to get back to doing the activity that made you successful. Or you can quit. It is very easy to want to walk away when you have no activity; the locomotive has stopped and you have no money coming. You are not sure when income will arrive. Even if you went out to work today, it's very unlikely you would get a check on Friday. You cannot get the locomotive of sales activity going from a dead stop in one day.

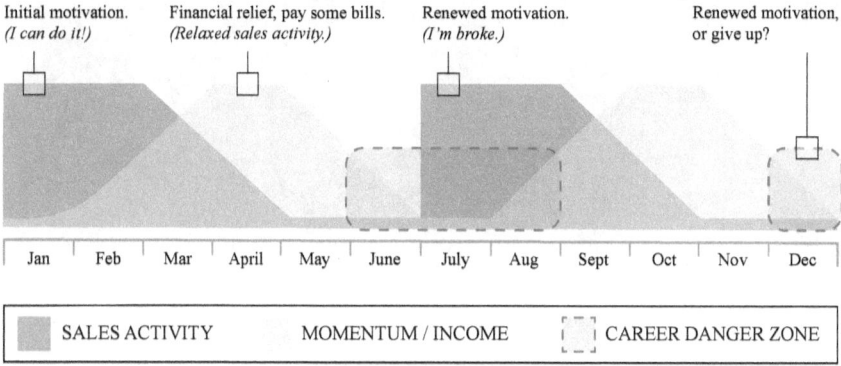

Figure 1.1

You must persist even when things are going good. This system is not a silver bullet where you go out and make calls and suddenly receive full gratification. What you will receive, in the short term, is evidence of progress. You will be able to measure the activity. You have been making contacts and using proven systems that have worked in the past. This allows sales people to hold their head high, knowing they are making progress. *Evidence of a job well done—not days filled with busy work—is the key you need to be able to press on.*

BENEFITING FROM THE SYSTEM

Even though activity today only results in deferred financial gratification, consistent use of the 20-Point System will serve you in the long term. Most people struggle with faith and persistence. This is actually a benefit to you. Higher compensation is demanded for jobs that most people cannot bring themselves to succeed at. If most people cannot, or will not, and you can and will, the market calls for high compensation.

"Successful people do what unsuccessful people are not willing to do. Don't wish it were easier; wish you were better." - *Jim Rohn*

CHAPTER 2

Instilling Faith

There are two ways to build faith that you are on the right track using the 20-Point System. This is an important part of the process because even though your company has proven systems, you may not be following them or you may be making critical mistakes, due to lack of training, lack of practice, or arrogance that you know better how to do the job. You need to:

1. **Review your sales process** with your manager, recruiter, or another experienced, and successful salesperson in your company.
2. **Keep track of your ratios** over a long period (minimum of 3-6 months).

PROCESS QUALITY CONTROL

If you are working the 20-Point System daily, you need to be sure that your process is sound. How are you approaching your customer? What is your phone script? What about your information gathering, presentation of solutions, and products? These need to be reviewed by someone who has experience in your field. This is usually the person who hired you. They are most likely being compensated for your sales performance and have a vested interest in your success. If there is no one like that available, seek out another successful person in your industry. Approach them with the appropriate humility for your inexperience and acknowledge their success. Most salespeople received help in their career and are willing to reciprocate if you are humble and offer to buy them breakfast or lunch.

RATIOS

The second way of instilling faith is by keeping track of your ratios: knowing how many times you ask a customer for a meeting vs. how many meetings you have or knowing how many meetings you actually have vs. how many sales you make. You should be able to determine what an appropriate ratio is for setting appointments and closing sales. Your manager or another person in your industry should be able to help you if your company does not have established guidelines for these ratios.

If you have taken one or both of these steps to ensure that your process is sound, you are ready to grind it out. Call on customers with faith and persistence, knowing that if you are getting 20 points per day, you will have money to pay your bills.

DRY SPELLS

Occasionally, a unique situation occurs. Because sales have a law of ratios, you can potentially have a stretch of time where you do not close much, or any, business. This is a naturally occurring event, and should not cause anxiety, although it always does. In my experience, if I have been doing my job faithfully and using the processes that work, a landslide of new business pours in following a dry spell.

Many times the customers I find during a dry spell were not even on my radar! There is no logical explanation for this occurrence, but with faith and persistence, you will find it to be true. Once you've seen it happen, you can depend on it with certainty in the future if you work your established process using the 20-Point System.

So here is what to expect with the 20-Point System:

1. No immediate financial gratification
2. Measurable activity resulting in future income
3. The need for reinforcement of logical sales processes
4. The need for faith and persistence
5. Expectation of dry spells

CHAPTER 3

The Calls

ONE OR TWO POINTS: ASKING FOR AN APPOINTMENT

There are really only two things that you can do that will generate points for you in the 20-Point System: asking for an appointment or having a scheduled appointment. Now that seems very simple, but there are rules to the system that will guard you from not awarding yourself points for unproductive behavior.

So let's define what validates giving yourself either one or two points and what is not included in this system at all. We don't want anyone fooling themselves into thinking they're being productive. There are many communication mediums that could be used to ask for a meeting:

1. Telephone
2. Face to face (in person)
3. Email (not recommended for initial contacts)
4. Text messages
5. Facebook Messenger
6. And many other mobile and online communication methods

There need to be some prerequisites to determine if this "ask" that you are doing is legitimately for business purposes *and* to move you closer to a sale.

You need to have a script and a goal (set a meeting) when you're asking someone to meet with you to talk about business. You are looking for an opportunity to present your products or services or an opportunity to present your proposals. You are trying to use your process so you can potentially close a sale.

One of the first things, is you need to be pre-sale with this prospect.

1. If it is a client who has already done business with you and now you need to deliver the product, this is not a pre-sale meeting.
2. If you have a follow up appointment that won't result in any kind of business, you get no points.
3. If there is no sale in the *near* future, then these calls do not give you any points.

You only earn points for pre-sale calls when talking to people that could potentially do business with you in the next 30 days. If these people cannot do business with you in the next 30 days, then it doesn't count towards getting one or two points.

> You need to ask for the appointment on the basis of business.

If you have some reason to believe that they can do business with you but not for a month or two, call them in a month or two. There is nothing more unattractive than an overeager sales person who wastes time going to meet with a prospect knowing he cannot close business. The customer will still be around in two months. A passive approach, and following up in two months, will seem much more professional.

ASKING FOR THE APPOINTMENT

You need to ask for the appointment on the basis of business. You need to say something along the lines of, "I was wondering if we could sit down so I can tell you a little bit about the type of work I do" or "I want to find out a little bit about how you are doing in the area of (your product/service)" or something similar so that the customer knows that you're meeting with them for the distinct purpose of talking about your product or service.

CASUAL LUNCH

Many sales people will call their personal market, their natural market, friends, and family, and they will try to convince them to get together to have lunch. They will arrange to go out for a beer or some other type of business networking meeting. Undisciplined salespeople will want to give themselves undeserved points or credit for having these appointments. Unless you're very specific on the phone about what you are intending to do when you meet with that prospect, you get no points.

You want to be able to start a dialogue towards the sale in this meeting. If you call someone and you get an answering machine, a wrong number, or they say it's not a good time and you don't get a chance to ask them for the appointment, none of those calls are worth any points.

The only thing that is actually worth 1 or 2 points is when you ask a potential customer if you can meet, it's pre-sale, and you have business purposes that you've clearly communicated to them. Period.

If you have clearly laid out why you are getting together, then you are doing your job. If this is unclear in any way and you wonder if you should give yourself points for something, don't. It is better to be conservative and earn the extra points than be liberal with points and cheat yourself.

If you put a business appointment on the calendar, you get two points. If you get told, "No" or "Call me back next week" or "This isn't a good time" after you have asked, then you get one point.

Getting one point is important. You have actually taken the time to do the activity where you <u>can</u> get rejected. Sales is a process of ratios. A certain percentage of people that you ask will agree to an appointment. You are moving yourself closer to getting those appointments. Even if you only get one point and you get told no, it is okay. If people tell you no, you are still getting closer to being able to go home for the day by getting your 20 points.

CHAPTER 4

Bad Days

3 POINTS: GETTING STOOD UP

Getting stood up is a bizarre reason for giving yourself points. Many people find it humorous that you can take credit for getting stiffed. This part of the 20-Point System is important. Getting stood up for appointments not only builds character; being stood up for appointments shows that you are out there trying.

People do not stand others up for a social visit nearly as often as they will for a sales call. If you are getting stood up a lot though, you definitely want to take a look at who your prospects are and examine your approach.

Are you being clear about:

1. Where you are supposed to meet?
2. The time?
3. The purpose of the meeting?

Have you confirmed your appointments? It is easy to shoot a text message to someone to confirm in advance. If you are being stood up more than once a week, it is clear that your value proposition for the customer is not strong enough or you are appearing to be unattractive to meet with. You will want to review your strategy with your manager, supervisor, or someone else successful in your industry.

Most of the time, when you talk to people about meeting with you for business and then they stand you up, it is because of a few possible reasons:

1. People can be flaky or inconsiderate (don't care).
2. People can be irresponsible (forgot).
3. An emergency came up.

There are very few emergencies, but occasionally they do happen. So always assume initially that someone had an emergency that came up and never lash out at people or become frustrated. Always just assume something happened and call them back to try and find out what's going on. I like to ask them if they are ok. Let them know you were worried that something might have happened to them.

Here are some scenarios that you will run into:

1. Someone reschedules prior to your appointment. They call, they say they can't make it, you ask if they can reschedule, and you put them on the calendar for a different day. **2 points**
2. If they call after the beginning of the appointment time or you call them, you were already stood up. **3 points**
3. If they reschedule after the appointment time, take the three points for being stood up and two for rescheduling. **5 points**
4. If they will not reschedule even if they promise to call you back to do so, you still get the three for being stood up and one for asking and being told no. **4 points**
5. If they call before the appointment and strictly cancel, you don't get any points for that day. **0 points**

GETTING PORCHED

My favorite term for being stood up at someone's house is *getting porched*. *Porched* is when you are standing on the porch, knocking on the door, and no one comes to the door. They're not home. Or, even worse, they're home and they won't answer the door. It's just you and the porch. Sometimes, you are at your office or meeting location, like a restaurant, and the client just doesn't show up. It definitely has happened to me before, and if it happens to you, don't feel bad. If you want to eat, eat. And if you want to just leave, pay for your drink and leave. It won't be the first time that someone has been seated at a restaurant and the other party has canceled or never arrives. This happens. If you have called them on their cell phone and they don't answer, wait 15 minutes, and if they don't show up or call back, you can leave. Try to reach them the next day if they don't call you.

If the person that stood you up finally gets a hold of you and you reschedule after you were stood up, you get three points for wasting your time. If they feel bad, apologize, and reschedule with you, not only do you get three points for getting stood up, you also receive two points for rescheduling the appointment for a different day. I have done a ton of business with people after they have stood me up. Most people feel awful about standing me up (as they should), and they're actually more likely to reschedule the next appointment and show up to that one. They are also more likely to do business. They feel like now they owe you something. If you think it through, maybe it's not so bizarre to award three points for being stood up. You have a potential customer who wasted your time and may want to try and make it up to you.

Most people feel awful about standing me up (as they should).

Do not get angry. Do not be flustered when you are stood up for appointments. It happens to everyone in sales. It will happen to you more when you're new in business and less when you are further in your career. Even though I am rarely stood up now, I still try and contact customers a couple of hours before my appointment and confirm that they're going to be coming in. Or I'll have my assistant call them and confirm that they're still coming in, especially if I scheduled the appointment a week or two earlier.

CHAPTER 5

Inevitable Circumstances

4 OR 5 POINTS: SCHEDULED APPOINTMENTS

The second activity that you perform to earn points in the 20-Point System involves meeting with prospective customers. This could be a current client or customer who has the potential to purchase more of your product or service, or it could be a new prospect. Of course, your client or prospect must keep the appointment. When you meet with them to either gather or present information about your product or service or finalize a sale, you must have the courage to lead the conversation towards the products and services you think may be appropriate.

TRANSITIONING TO A SALES APPOINTMENT

If you are in sales, you will likely find yourself in a situation where you are meeting with someone and you did not disclose to up front that you want to talk about your product or service. This usually happens for one of two reasons: you had dual purposes to meet or you were scared to mention your business motives because of fear of rejection. Even though the goal on the phone is to schedule appointments, be sure to be clear about your motives so you can eliminate people who are not interested quickly. You are going to want to take points for this meeting though, so ask the person if they wouldn't mind talking about your product or service. They might be a bit annoyed or feel like you pulled the "bait and switch"—and you did (not good). But as Wayne Gretzke said, "You miss 100% of the shots you don't take." So ask for permission and transition to discussing business so your time isn't wasted networking. If you're not asking questions and discussing your services, then you're not in a sales appointment: you're in a socializing appointment or networking appointment. You receive no points.

Once you determine that you're in a sales appointment, if you don't close the sale, you receive four points. It is entirely possible that you planned to not try and close the sale at this meeting. Many times, I meet with a customer and tell them that they are in an information-gathering meeting. I plan to gather information from them, ask questions, and I will then prepare recommendations for the following meeting. You receive 4 points.

If you were planning to close the sale, you may get to a point where you cannot continue. Possibly, the client or customer doesn't want to continue with the process for one reason or another. The prospect may raise an objection that you cannot overcome, or they may delay your request to move forward. Whatever the reason for not moving forward, you only receive four points. If you think there is still the possibility that they are going to do business with you, try to schedule the next event that will move the process forward. If they say no or that they will get back to you, you get one point. If you are able to schedule the follow-up appointment, you receive 2 points.

Make sure you do your whole job at the meeting if you are awarding yourself four points. If you are selling a product or service that should be sold in one meeting, such as selling candles, offering cosmetics, showing houses, or leasing equipment, you should be asking them if they are interested in placing an order, writing an offer, or putting down a deposit. If the meeting involved you reviewing the benefits of your product or service, you should be asking for the sale. Earning four points assumes that you are doing everything possible to move forward with the process. Do not leave the appointment unfinished or be sheepish with your process. Do not feed your clients objections like, "Why don't you think it over." *Ask for the sale.* Awarding yourself points for a poor process will not allow for an accurate measurement of your activity.

One of the things that might happen in an initial appointment is you may come to the conclusion that the person you are talking with is not a good potential customer for you. Possibly it's just bad timing, or maybe they will never make a good customer. You will meet people who:

» have personality differences with you,

» you don't like,

» don't like you,

» are broke, or

» don't have interest or need in your product or service.

Regardless why the person isn't a good prospect, you did a good enough job with your prospect to determine this, and you should not proceed. You still get four points for the meeting. You should not be setting a second appointment. Let the person know that if their situation changes, they are welcome to contact you and you would love to potentially work with them in the future. If you think they could be a good prospect but they just are not right now, you could ask if you could put them in the calendar to follow up in six months or a year. This will allow you to have a pipeline of potential prospects to call on in the future.

It is very important for you and the prospect to identify that they are not a good potential customer right now. You do not want to waste your time. You could boldly ask them, "Does it make sense for us to continue talking about this right now?" You need to identify exactly what product or service you will be able to recommend to your potential customer. If you cannot identify a product or service for them to buy, then you should not be meeting with them again. I have had customers who were eager to go forward in the process, and I literally listed my products and services to them and asked them if any were a fit so they could clearly see why we should no longer meet. Sometimes people will be so kind and continually allow you to think there is a possibility of a sale. Unless you are frank with them, they won't say no. Occasionally, you have to tell people that they need to call you when their situation changes.

5 POINTS: CLOSING BUSINESS

Closing business should not be too difficult to define. For this, you earn five points. Everything must be finalized though. You must have collected the check, completed the paperwork, placed the order, closed the deal, or delivered the product. This is different in various industries. If you can say to the customer, "Thank you for the business." You have closed the sale. If you still need something (like the check), then you will only take four points that day.

KEEPING TRACK

When I am keeping track of my 20 points, it's very simple. Usually, I use a yellow note pad to list the people I need to call and the tasks I need to accomplish. At the top of that page, I write:

» N -   » A -
» Y -   » S -
» S -

This stands for "No," "Yes," "Stood," "Appointment," and "Sale." I start tallying up my points as I make phone calls or have my appointments for the day. If you have no appointments scheduled for the day, then you better have a big section of your day planned out for phoning. That is the only way you're going to generate any points.

» N - 1,1,1   » A - 4
» Y - 2,2   » S - 5
» S -

If you get to 3 pm and your points look like this, you have to make some phone calls, unless you have another scheduled appointment. When you are planning your day, it's good to look at your scheduled appointments and then plan the time for making calls, knowing you may only have two scheduled meetings.

Keeping track is easy: you can use scratch paper, you can put it on your calendar, or you can use the 20-point sheet that is downloadable from 20pointsystem.com. I like to use a magnetic monthly calendar to keep track of the days that I hit 20. I put magnetic markers on the days I achieve my 20 points. With a monthly calendar, I can look back and have confidence when I see many markers showing high levels of activity. Even if you don't get your 20 points done every single day, knowing that you have hit your goal most days is motivating. You are most likely having more progress than you were having before you started tracking your activity.

CHAPTER 6

Conclusion

The most important thing about the 20-Point System is being honest with yourself. The more conservative you are about giving yourself points when you legitimately earned them, the better. If you are really out on a social call but give yourself points for it, you are only cheating yourself. When you ask for an appointment that could become a sale or you have an appointment scheduled that was designed to be a sales appointment, you should be proud of your accomplishment. Sales are not consistent, and you do not know how every situation will work out. What you can control is your activity and process.

Even though you have consistency, there are other ways you can ruin your sales career. If you dress poorly, speak poorly, have poor hygiene, or have other bad habits, these things can sabotage your sales career regardless of how many points you get. Make sure you are getting constant feedback from people you trust. But if you're doing most of the other things right, the 20-Point System is a way for you to know that when you get your 20 Points, you can go home. You have done enough, and you can have dinner and be with your family. You can go to sleep and not stress because a month or two from now, you're going to have income from your efforts.

If you already have successful processes in your sales career and you apply this 20-Point System to your daily activity, your success will increase. There is no question. Do more consistently; what you already know works. Your biggest benefit is to stay off the income roller coaster. You don't want the highs and lows of taking weeks off and then running like crazy to catch up.

Do the appropriate amount of sales activity on a daily basis and keep track of it with the 20-Point System. Just like the locomotive, it won't take off quickly. It is a lot of work shoveling all that coal into the boiler. Once you build some momentum though, just like the locomotive, it is *powerful*.